I went for a walk. I passed a stone wall
and saw something move.
What could it be?

Ladybugs.

I passed a wood fence
and saw something move.
What could it be?

Snails.

I passed wild roses
and saw something move.
What could it be?

Caterpillars.

I passed a wood pile
and saw something move.
What could it be?

Ants.

I passed some purple thistles
and saw something move.
What could it be?

A bee.

I passed some tall grass
and saw something move.
What could it be?

A spider.

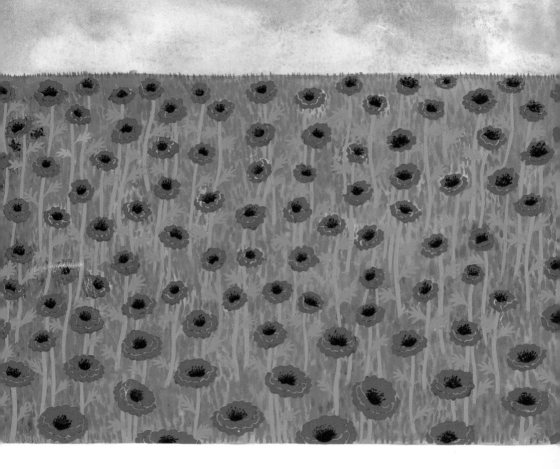

I passed a poppy field
and saw something move.
What could it be?

Butterflies.

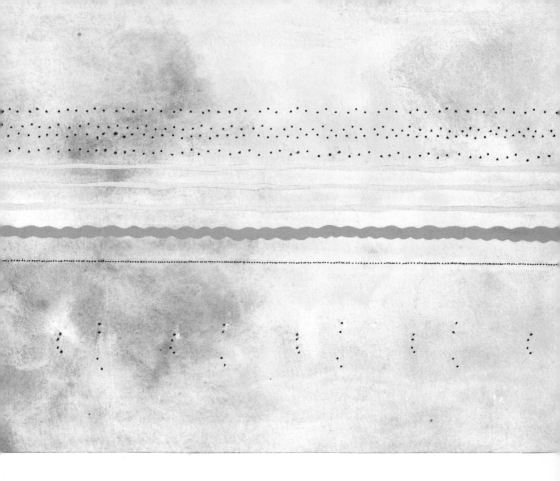

Now what could these be?

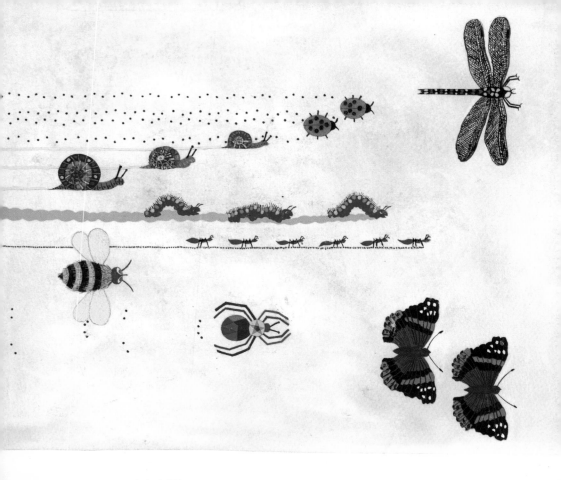

Ah! They are all going home —
just like me.